# It's Time To Brush My Teeth

To Iva with love,
Mommy

Brush

To request permissions, contact the Author at healthysmilezone@gmail.com or visit www.healthysmilezone.com

Paperback ISBN: 978-0-6451502-0-9
Ebook ISBN: 978-0-6451502-1-6

First paperback edition April 2021

Author: Yana Saranchova
Illustrator: Khadija Maryam

Published by Kindle Direct Publishing in the USA

# It's Time To Brush My Teeth

Written by
## Yana Saranchova

Illustrated by
## Khadija Maryam

Every night after dinner, little Iva and her rabbit Bobo were too lazy to brush their teeth. They would leave their tooth brushing routine until the very last minute, and sometimes they would forget to brush altogether. They did not listen to Mommy when she kept telling them to brush their teeth twice a day, once in the morning and once in the evening, to keep their teeth healthy. Instead, they had a million excuses not to brush their teeth since they were too busy running around playing with their favorite toys.

One day, in the morning, Iva woke up in pain.

"Ow Ow!" screamed Iva.

"What is wrong?" asked Bobo.

"My tooth hurts!" said Iva. "It must be from not brushing my teeth before bed and after eating all those sweets for dinner!"

"Oh no, what should we do?" asked Bobo.

"We must tell Mommy," said Iva. "She will find a way to help us."

"Mommy, I'm sorry I should've listened to you and brushed my teeth before bed," said Iva. "Now, I have a toothache!"

"Open your mouth and let me take a look," said Mommy. "Oh dear, looks like you have a black hole in your tooth known as a cavity and it is filled with cavity monsters."

"Yuck!" said Bobo. "Are cavity monsters bad for you?"

"Well, if you don't brush them off, they will eat the leftovers of your food stuck in between your teeth, and sometimes if they are starving, they can also eat through your tooth as well," said Mommy.

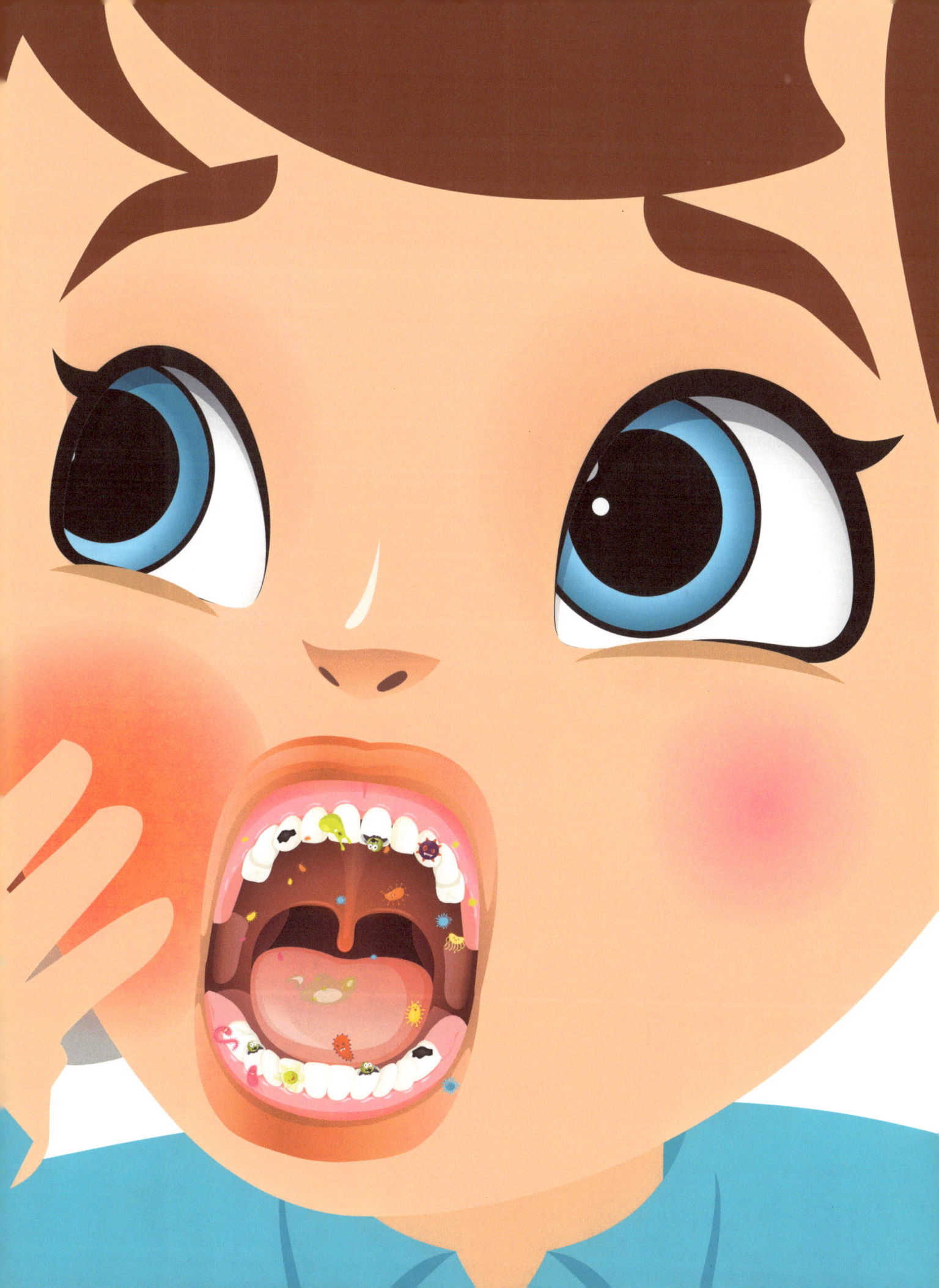

"Mommy, what kind of food do cavity monsters like to eat?" asked Iva.

"Oh, I know, I know," said Bobo. "They like sweets, sugary drinks, gummy candies, chips, crackers, and french fries."

"That is correct," said Mommy. "These sweet foods are known as carbohydrates."

"Oh no, but that is my favorite type of food," said Iva.

"Mine too!" said Bobo.

"It is okay to eat that type of food in small quantities and as long as you brush your teeth afterwards," said Mommy.

# FOODS BAD FOR TEETH

CARBOHYDRATES

"Mommy, can you also tell me which foods are good for my teeth so I can eat more of them," said Iva.

"I heard that crunchy fruits and vegetables are good for your teeth," said Bobo.

"That's right, Bobo," said Mommy. "If you want your teeth to stay healthy, you should eat more carrots, celery, broccoli, cucumbers, apples, bananas, as well as milk products. Examples of milk products are cheese, milk, and yogurt. Also, you should drink plenty of water in between."

"So how can we make my tooth healthy again?" asked Iva.

"By visiting the dentist," replied Mommy. "He will rescue your tooth!"

# FOODS GOOD FOR TEETH

Yogurt

Milk

"Hi, I'm Dr. Filler, the local dentist," introduced himself, Dr. Filler. "Come take a seat in my special chair and put on these super cool glasses to protect your eyes. In the meantime, I will get a tooth camera to take a tooth picture."

"I like this chair," said Iva. "It goes up and down like a theme park ride."

"Iva, let's play a game," said Dr. Filler. "If you can stay still and keep your mouth open until I finish fixing your tooth, then I'll give you a prize."

"I want to play too!" said Bobo.

Welcome to
Dr. Filler's Office

"Is this wide enough?" asked Iva after she opened her mouth as wide as possible.

"That is perfect!" said Dr. Filler. "First, I will use my little mirror and a bright light to look deep down into your tooth hole. Then, I will get rid of all of the nasty cavity monsters, so they don't keep digging a bigger cavity monster cave in the tooth. Finally, I will put some white material in the hole to make the tooth look brand new and healthy."

"I am scared!" said Iva. "Is my tooth going to feel any pain?"

"Don't worry little one," said Dr. Filler. "You shouldn't be scared; it is the cavity monsters that should be scared. I will put your tooth to sleep with my magic gel so that when the tooth wakes up, it won't even realize it had a filling."

"Dr. Filler, what do teeth look like on the inside?" asked Bobo.

"That is an excellent question," said Dr. Filler. "Each tooth has two parts: a visible white part above the gums known as a crown, and an invisible part below the gums known as a root. The crown of a tooth is like an apple. An apple has an outer skin and inner flesh to protect the seeds. Similarly, the tooth crown also has an outer enamel and inner dentine to protect the pulp. The outer enamel is the hardest material in your body. The middle layer, dentine, is made up of tiny tubules. While the pulp has nerves in it, causing you to feel pain when the cavity monsters eat through your tooth. You can stop cavity monsters from getting inside your tooth simply by brushing your teeth."

# TOOTH ANATOMY

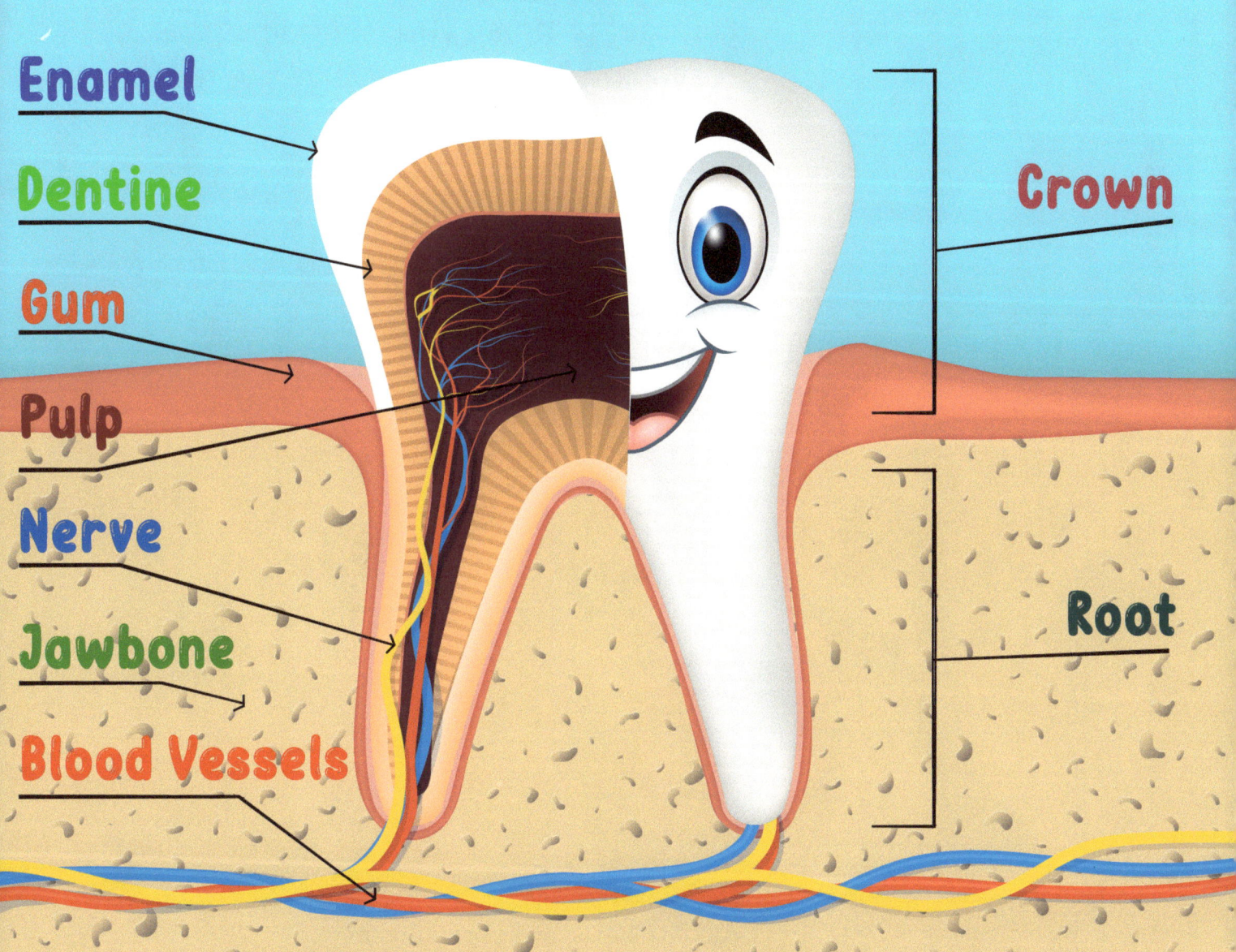

Enamel

Dentine

Gum

Pulp

Nerve

Jawbone

Blood Vessels

Crown

Root

"Dr. Filler, but I don't know how to brush my teeth," said Iva.

"That's okay; I can teach you," said Dr. Filler. "Just follow these eight easy steps."

Step 1: Wet your toothbrush.

Step 2: Apply only a pea-sized amount of toothpaste onto your toothbrush.

Step 3: Smile and brush your teeth up and down and round and round for 2 minutes twice a day.

Step 4: Don't forget to brush your tongue as well.

Step 5: Don't swallow the toothpaste. Make sure to spit it out.

Step 6: Turn off the water.

Step 7: Put your brush where it belongs.

Step 8: After you brush your teeth then it is time to floss. Flossing is how you clean in between your teeth and gums.

Step 1

Step 2

Step 3

Step 4

Step 5

Step 6

Step 7

Step 8

"There is an even easier way to learn how to brush your teeth," said Dr. Filler. "It is by learning this song."

"Let's sing together!" said Bobo.

Brush, brush. It's time to brush your teeth.
Yes, yes, yes, I want to brush my teeth.
Good, good, brushing is good for you.
Yay yay yay takes only 2 minutes wooh!

Here comes the water, here comes the brush.
Here comes the pea-sized paste for your brush.
Zoom, zoom up and down your teeth,
As you brush twice a day to the beat!

One, two, three, germs are gone, you see.
Yes, yes, yes, you did a great job, WOW!
Brush, brush, brush, they're all CLEAN now!

"Thank you for saving my tooth," said Iva. "It no longer hurts!"

"You are most welcome," said Dr. Filler. "Here is a little prize for you for being brave and keeping your mouth wide open for such a long time."

"Wow!" said Iva. "My very own light-up flashing toothbrush with a timer! Thank you again, Dr. Filler."

"Here is one for you as well, Bobo," said Dr. Filler. "Teeth are important for chewing, speaking, and smiling, so make sure to take care of them with the use of these toothbrushes."

"You're the best," exclaimed Bobo.

That night, the first thing Iva and Bobo did after dinner was race to the bathroom to brush their teeth. They knew better now than to not brush their teeth before bedtime.

"I just finished brushing my teeth for the full two minutes," said Iva.

"Wow, your teeth look so clean and shiny," said Bobo.

"Yes, I don't want cavity monsters to be building another cavity monster cave in my tooth," said Iva. "So from now on, I will always brush my teeth twice a day."

"Good idea," said Bobo. "Also, let's not forget to visit the dentist every 6 months for regular checkups."

"I agree, let's not forget!" said Iva. "Visiting Dr. Filler was so much fun."

# BRUSHING TOOLS

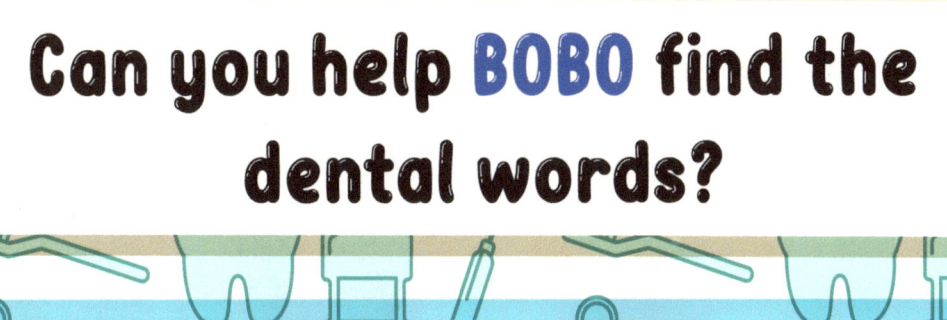

```
Y  R  R  A  L  H  S  H
D  E  N  T  I  S  T  Y
M  S  B  O  R  O  A  S
O  M  O  O  O  M  S  B
L  I  A  T  R  O  C  R
A  L  H  H  L  U  S  U
R  E  M  F  L  O  S  S
C  H  E  C  K  U  P  H
```

**Dentist**    **Checkup**    **Tooth**    **Molar**

**Brush**    **Smile**    **Floss**

# Can you help IVA find her brushing tools through the tooth maze?

START

FINISH

# BRUSHING SCHEDULE

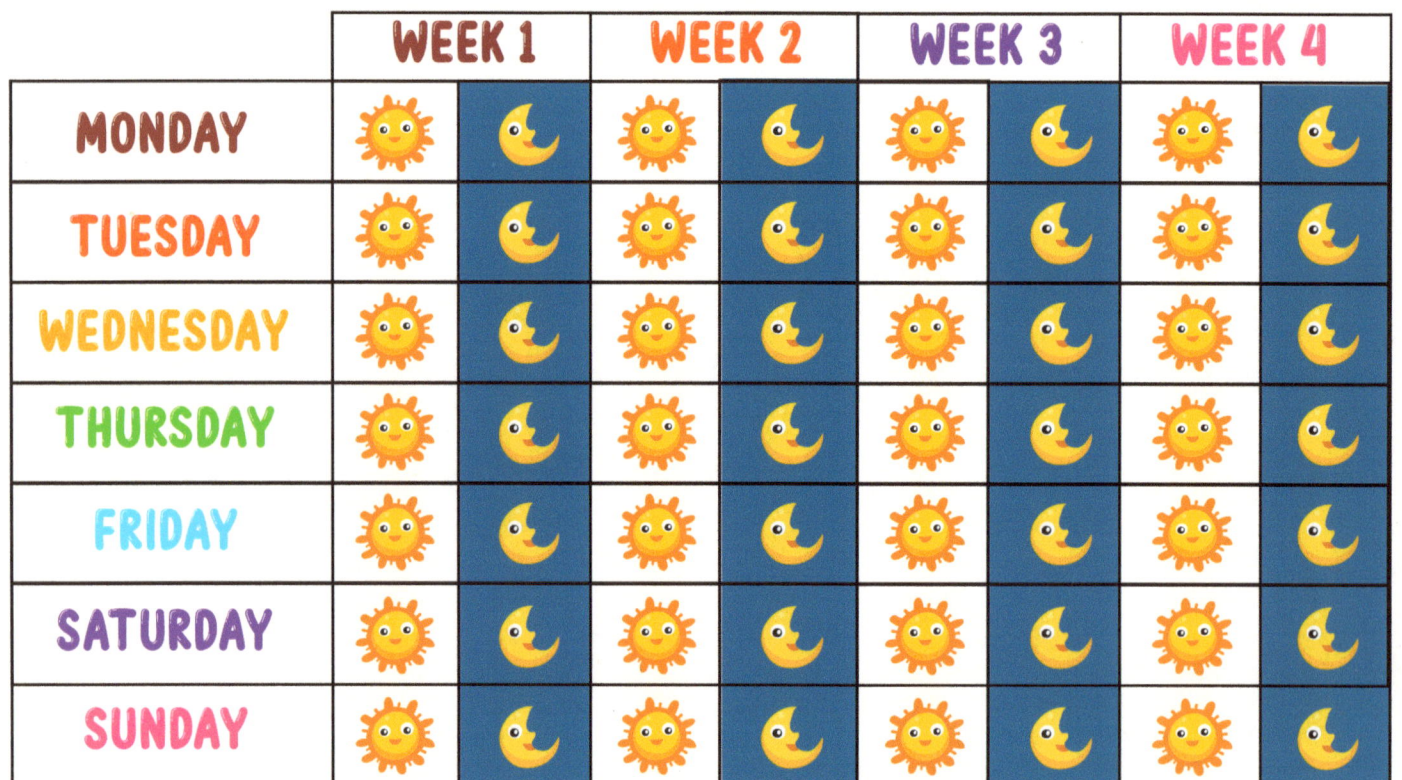

I Brushed Two Times Today!

| | WEEK 1 | | WEEK 2 | | WEEK 3 | | WEEK 4 | |
|---|---|---|---|---|---|---|---|---|
| MONDAY | ☀️ | 🌙 | ☀️ | 🌙 | ☀️ | 🌙 | ☀️ | 🌙 |
| TUESDAY | ☀️ | 🌙 | ☀️ | 🌙 | ☀️ | 🌙 | ☀️ | 🌙 |
| WEDNESDAY | ☀️ | 🌙 | ☀️ | 🌙 | ☀️ | 🌙 | ☀️ | 🌙 |
| THURSDAY | ☀️ | 🌙 | ☀️ | 🌙 | ☀️ | 🌙 | ☀️ | 🌙 |
| FRIDAY | ☀️ | 🌙 | ☀️ | 🌙 | ☀️ | 🌙 | ☀️ | 🌙 |
| SATURDAY | ☀️ | 🌙 | ☀️ | 🌙 | ☀️ | 🌙 | ☀️ | 🌙 |
| SUNDAY | ☀️ | 🌙 | ☀️ | 🌙 | ☀️ | 🌙 | ☀️ | 🌙 |

# FUN FACTS ABOUT DENTISTRY FOR CHILDREN

- 700 types of species of bacteria live in the mouth.

- There are 100 billion bacteria in your mouth.

- Soft drinks, juices, and any other acidic drinks wear away the enamel that protects the teeth.

- Tooth enamel is the hardest substance in the body.

- Baby teeth are already in your jaw the moment you are born.

- You exert about 200lb of pressure when you bite down.

- Children have 20 baby teeth that fall out and are replaced by 32 permanent adult teeth.

- People spend about 38.5 days brushing their teeth over a lifetime.

- If you don't floss, you miss roughly 40% of tooth surfaces.

- Two-thirds of your tooth is hidden underneath your gums.

- When brushing teeth, toothpaste should be spat out without rinsing the mouth with water.

- We would not be able to taste anything without saliva.

- Tongue is the strongest muscle in your body.

- Mosquitos have 47 teeth that are used not for chewing but for attaching to your skin.

- A person produces enough saliva to fill two swimming pools over a lifetime.

# FUN FACTS ABOUT DENTISTRY FOR ADULTS

- Children under 18 months should not use toothpaste with fluoride.

- Children between 18 months and 6 years should use 500-550ppm fluoride-containing toothpaste.

- Children above the age of 6 should use 1000-1500ppm fluoride-containing toothpaste.

- Children under the age of 6 should not use fluoride mouthrinse.

- Fluoride gel should not be used under the age of 10.

- Fluoride varnish can be used for children under the age of 10.

- Dry mouth can cause bad breath.

- Calculus can only be removed with special instruments at the dental office and cannot be removed with regular brushing.

- Take your baby to the dentist when their first tooth comes out or when they become 12 months old (whichever comes first).

- Most bacteria are not brushed off around gums and in between teeth.

Printed in Australia
AUHW011140210122
358585AU00002B/3